Nevada Public Library
631 K Avenue
Nevada, IA 50201
515-382-2628

WHITE HOUSE INSIDERS

What's It Like to Be the
PRESIDENT'S KID?

BY KATHLEEN CONNORS

Gareth Stevens
PUBLISHING

Please visit our website, www.garethstevens.com. For a free color catalog of all our high-quality books, call toll free 1-800-542-2595 or fax 1-877-542-2596.

Library of Congress Cataloging-in-Publication Data

Connors, Kathleen.
What's it like to be the President's kid? / by Kathleen Connors.
p. cm. — (White House insiders)
Includes index.
ISBN 978-1-4824-1101-0 (pbk.)
ISBN 978-1-4824-1102-7 (6-pack)
ISBN 978-1-4824-1100-3 (library binding)
1. Children of presidents — United States — Juvenile literature. 2. Children of presidents — United States — Biography — Juvenile literature. I. Connors, Kathleen. II. Title.
E176.45 C66 2014
973.09—d23

First Edition

Published in 2015 by
Gareth Stevens Publishing
111 East 14th Street, Suite 349
New York, NY 10003

Copyright © 2015 Gareth Stevens Publishing

Designer: Nick Domiano
Editor: Kristen Rajczak

Photo credits: Cover, p. 1 (Jenna Bush) Charles Eshelman/FilmMagic/Getty Images; cover, p. 1 (Sasha and Malia Obama) Jewel Samad/AFP/Getty Images; cover, p. 1 (Chelsea Clinton) Dimitrios Kambouris/Getty Images Entertainment/Getty Images; p. 5 Ramin Talaie/Getty Images News/Getty Images; p. 7 Michael Geissinger/Time & Life Pictures/Getty Images; p. 9 Paul Schutzer/Time & Life Pictures/Getty Images; p. 11 Paul Hawthorne/Getty Images Entertainment/Getty Images; p. 13 Dan Farrell/NY Daily News Archive via Getty Images; p. 15 Kevin Mazur/WireImage/Getty Images; p. 17 Luke Frazza/AFP/Getty Images; p. 19 David Hume Kennerly/Hulton Archive/Getty Images.

Printed in the United States of America

CPSIA compliance information: Batch #CS15GS: For further information contact Gareth Stevens, New York, New York at 1-800-542-2595.

Contents

Words in the glossary appear in **bold** type the first time they are used in the text.

Are They Like You?

The president's children live in the East Wing of the White House with their family. Their breakfast is made by one of the professional chefs that work there. Susan Ford, daughter of President Gerald Ford, has said, "You can be waited on hand and foot if you want that."

Even with all these **privileges**, children of the president are a lot more like you than you think. Susan said her mom still told her to make her own bed!

The Inside Scoop

Esther Cleveland was the only president's child born inside the White House. She was born in September 1893 after her father, Grover Cleveland, was elected to his second presidential term.

Presidents' kids often have the chance to meet well-known people and characters. Here, President Bill Clinton's daughter, Chelsea, speaks with Rosita from *Sesame Street* at a meeting in 2013.

Not All "Kids"

The US **Constitution** states that the president must be at least 35 years old to be elected. However, most presidents have been much older than that. This means that many of the presidents' children were already grown up and never lived in the White House.

To date, Ronald Reagan was the oldest president to be elected at age 69. President Reagan's oldest daughter, Maureen, was 39 when her father took office in 1980. Ronald Jr., the youngest of the five Reagan children, was 22.

The Inside Scoop

Julie Nixon was in college when her father, Richard Nixon, was president. Despite her age, she has said, "Once you've been a White House kid, you'll always be a White House kid. It's always part of you."

A number of president's children have been married at the White House! In 1967, Lynda Bird Johnson's wedding was held in the East Room of the White House while her father, Lyndon Johnson, was president.

7

Young Families

Historically, it's been rare for young children to live at the White House. Maybe that's why it's so fun to think of what their lives would have been like!

Caroline Kennedy was only 3 years old when she moved into the White House with her family in 1960. Her younger brother, John Jr., was just a baby. Nine-year-old Amy Carter was President Jimmy Carter's youngest child. When he took office, Amy's three older brothers already lived on their own.

The Inside Scoop

Malia and Sasha Obama were the youngest president's children to move into the White House since the Kennedys. Malia was 10 and Sasha was 7 when they moved in.

The lives of President John F. Kennedy's children Caroline and John Jr. were of great interest to the American people. That's often the case with young presidents' children.

Stay in School

If one of your parents were president, you'd still have to go to school! Presidents' kids don't all go to the same school, though. Tad and Willie Lincoln had **tutors** that came to the White House. So did President Rutherford B. Hayes's kids, Scott and Fanny Hayes.

Recent presidents' kids have gone to schools nearby. Amy Carter attended a public school in Washington, DC. Susan Ford, who was 17 when her father became president, went to a private school called the Holton Arms School.

The Inside Scoop

Many presidents' kids had dogs—but President Teddy Roosevelt's six children had a pony and a macaw in addition to cats and dogs!

While their father, George W. Bush, was in office, Jenna and Barbara Bush went to college. Barbara (right) attended Yale University, and Jenna (left) went to the University of Texas at Austin.

Safety First

The president's kids, along with the rest of the First Family, have a Secret Service team to keep them safe at all times. The Secret Service goes with them to school and is even close by if they're just playing in their bedroom.

Having **security** around you all the time can be annoying. Susan Ford once dodged her Secret Service agents and drove right out the White House gates. Later, she said, "Everybody tries it. It becomes a challenge, and you want to succeed."

The Inside Scoop

The members of the First Family have code names given by the Secret Service. President Lyndon Johnson's daughter Lynda's code name was "Velvet."

Some president's kids have said they felt lonely or **isolated** partly because of the constant presence of the Secret Service. In pictures like this one of Amy Carter (center), you can see Secret Service agents in the background wearing suits.

Making Mischief

Just because there's security around all the time doesn't mean the president's kids don't get into trouble! Quentin Roosevelt ran his wagon right through a valuable painting when his dad, Theodore Roosevelt, was president. Amy Carter's roller skates left marks all over the East Room's floor!

The president's kid is likely taught to watch what they say. But Caroline Kennedy once told reporters that her father was "upstairs with his shoes and socks off, not doing anything." Oops!

The Inside Scoop

Tad Lincoln was only 7 years old when he moved into the White House in 1861. He loved to play war, but once he went too far. Tad fired his toy cannon outside the **Cabinet** room while a meeting was in session!

Being the president's child means any real trouble you might get into can negatively affect the president. But often, a president's kids figure positively into the president's image.

15

Fun and Games

Being the president's kid has lots of benefits. The White House has an outdoor pool, basketball and tennis court, bowling alley, and movie theater. Margaret Truman watched one movie 16 times there!

The land around the White House is called President's Park, and all the trees and green grass make it like living in your own park. Amy Carter had a tree house on the South Lawn. It's also where the **annual** Easter Egg Roll, or hunt, is every spring.

The Inside Scoop

Depending on the age of the children, the president's kids sometimes have to attend fancy state dinners, speeches, and other political events. Amy Carter was excused from state dinners after she once brought a book to read!

One of the most fun yearly celebrations at the White House is the lighting of the national Christmas tree. Here, Chelsea Clinton (center) lights the tree with her parents, First Lady Hillary Clinton and President Bill Clinton.

'Round the World

In 2013, Sasha and Malia Obama went to Africa with their parents. They've also been to Paris, France, and Moscow, Russia. Lots of travel isn't uncommon. Modern presidents' kids have the chance to visit places all over the United States and throughout the world.

Travel is certainly a perk of being a president's kid. But often the president and First Lady travel without their children, too. Presidents' kids have to learn how to deal with their parents being far away often.

The Inside Scoop

Most presidents were **politicians** before taking office, so their children are already used to the busy calendar the president will have.

Many presidents talk about how hard it is to make time for their families while in office. Here, President Gerald Ford (second from right) and his family spend Christmas together in Colorado.

Media Coverage

Presidents have long asked reporters to keep their distance from younger children. However, that often doesn't stop them from taking lots of pictures of the president's kids when they're out at events.

Presidents' kids grow up in the spotlight, and their activities are always interesting to the American public. After they no longer live in the White House, some stay away from the **media** and try to have private lives. Others, such as Chelsea Clinton and Jenna Bush, have worked in the media as reporters themselves!

The Inside Scoop

Jacqueline Kennedy disliked the press so much she set up her daughter Caroline's whole class in a room at the White House so Caroline wouldn't have to go out for school.

First Kid Fun

- Tad Lincoln met the Union soldiers protecting the White House during the Civil War. He even wore a uniform matching theirs.

- Quentin Roosevelt's brothers brought his pony up to his bedroom using the White House elevator.

- As a small child, John Kennedy Jr. used to hide under President Kennedy's desk in the Oval Office. He sometimes had to be taken out in order for meetings to take place.

- Susan Ford found a big rolling cart of cookies in the White House kitchen. She stuffed her pockets full and ran back to her room.

- Steven Ford climbed on the White House roof to play the band Led Zeppelin on his stereo.

- On the night Bill Clinton was sworn in as president, the White House staff set up a **scavenger hunt** for Chelsea Clinton and her friends. They did it again for Malia and Sasha Obama in 2009!

Glossary

annual: occurring every year

Cabinet: a group of advisers chosen by the US president. They are also the heads of major government departments.

constitution: the basic laws by which a country or state is governed

isolated: the state of being alone

media: the outlets and people that offer news coverage

politician: a person who runs for or holds a government position

privilege: special treatment and benefits

scavenger hunt: a game in which the players have to find certain hidden objects

security: a group whose main job is keeping a place safe

tutor: a teacher who instructs an individual student

For More Information

BOOKS

Besel, Jennifer M. *Malia and Sasha Obama*. Mankato, MN: Capstone Press, 2011.

Rhatigan, Joe. *White House Kids: The Perks, Pleasures, Problems, and Pratfalls of the Presidents' Children*. Watertown, MA: Charlesbridge Publishing, 2012.

WEBSITES

All the President's Children
americanhistory.si.edu/presidency/5a2b.html
Play a game to learn fun facts about past presidents' kids.

An Album of Presidents and Their Children
content.time.com/time/photogallery/0,29307,1869753,00.html
Check out pictures of past presidents' kids.

Index